Adrienne Barman

PLANTOPEDIA

A CELEBRATION OF NATURE'S GREATEST SHOW-OFFS

WIDE EYED EDITIONS

Contents

PLANTOPEDIA celebrates the dazzling and diverse plants that grow on Planet Earth. Without plants, people wouldn't exist - they provide us with food and the materials we need to make things like plastic, clothes and houses. They even clean the air, giving us the oxygen we need to breathe. But sadly many plants are now under threat from farming, road-building, pollution and climate change.

Turn the page to meet nature's greatest show-offs and discover which plants are the biggest, stinkiest, most magical and most poisonous of all.

The air fresheners

Maranta

Sword fern Grows well in bathrooms.

Gerbera Grow these South African daisies in a cool, bright spot.

Flamingo flower Don't let pets eat this plant - it's poisonous!

The air fresheners

Queen of the night

Umbrella tree

Areca palm

House azaelea

Jade plant
Some people think this plant brings good luck.

The all-blacks

Bat flower A seriously spooky houseplant from Southeast Asia.

Tulip 'Queen of the night' Actually dark purple rather than black.

The all-blacks

Elderberry Use them to make jam.

Halfeti black rose Named after a town in Turkey, the only place where it grows naturally.

Dark rampion

Blackcurrant

Black calla lily

Black hollyhock

Viola 'Molly Sanderson'

The aquatics

Arrowhead

Watermeal Grab a magnifying glass, it's the world's smallest flowering plant.

Water moss

Bog arum Careful - this plant is toxic from root to tip!

Western marsh orchid

Watercress

Water mint

Yellow iris

Grows to over a metre tall.

Water chestnut

Water hyacinth

The aquatics

Alder Alder wood doesn't rot easily, so it's used to make boats.

Flowering rush

Marsh pennywort Turn over the floating leaves to find tiny pink flowers.

European white water lily

Weeping willow

Meadowsweet

Water crowfoot

Bulrush

Common eelgrass

Sugar kelp A sweet tasting seaweed that you can eat!

The big eaters

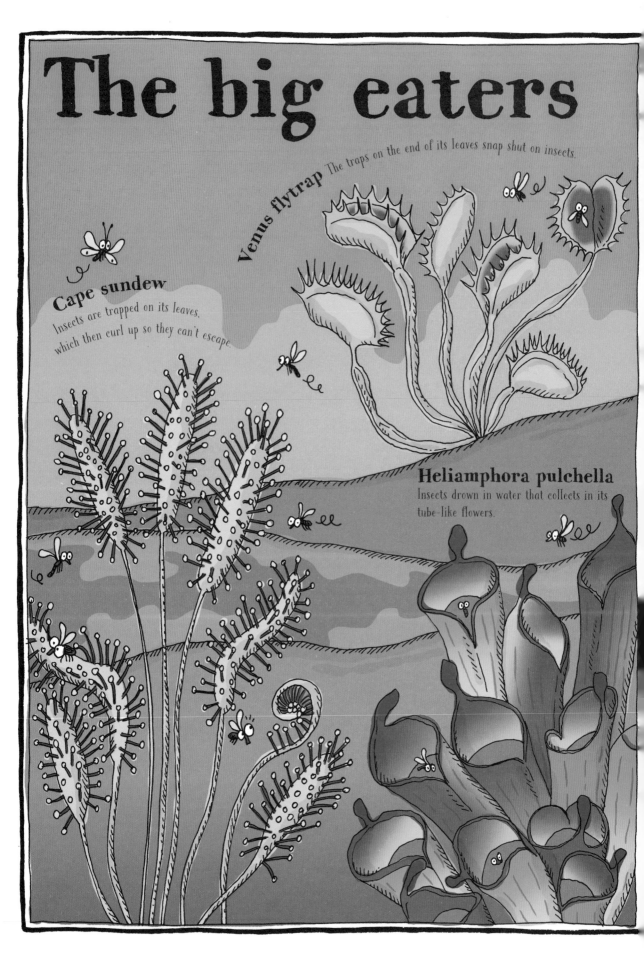

Venus flytrap The traps on the end of its leaves snap shut on insects.

Cape sundew
Insects are trapped on its leaves, which then curl up so they can't escape.

Heliamphora pulchella
Insects drown in water that collects in its tube-like flowers.

Yellow butterwort
Insects get trapped on its leaves.

Alpine butterwort
Mind the sticky leaves!

Greater bladderwort
Traps its prey underwater!

Irish butterwort
If you're an insect, avoid its sticky leaves!

Powdery strap airplant
Traps prey with its leaves.

The big eaters

Attenborough's pitcher plant
Insects drown in the water it collects.

Purple pitcher plant
Collects water in its flowers... and waits for insects to drown!

Brocchinia
Watch out for the water!

Round-leaved sundew
Sticky tendrils snap up insects.

The blues and purples

Jacaranda

Morning glory The flowers open in the morning and close at night.

Paulownia Paulownia wood is used to make musical instruments and surfboards.

Harebell

Beautyberry

Meadow clary

Sweet violet

Saffron crocus The spice saffron is made from crocus stamen.

Common passion flower

Viper's bugloss Bees love it!

Rosemary Delicious baked in bread or rubbed on roast lamb.

Annual lunar

Shallot
A bit like a little onion.

The cereals

Maize Also known as sweetcorn

Wheat First grown in the Middle East 10,000 years ago

Sorghum *Grows in Africa and Asia.*

Rice

Oats *Delicious as porridge!*

Millet

Spelt

Barley

Rye *Makes great bread*

Buckwheat

The citrus fruits

Lemon

Buddha's hand
Smells like a lemon, looks like no other fruit on Earth!

Seville orange
Makes delicious marmalade.

Lime

Orange

The citrus fruits

2

Mandarin

Yuzu

Kumquat
Not much larger than a strawberry.

Pomelo
Looks like a large grapefruit.

Citron Its rind is tastier than its fruit (if you coat it in sugar)!

Bergamot orange Used to make Earl Grey tea and perfume.

Clementine A cross between a sweet orange and a mandarin.

Grapefruit Grows in clusters like bunches of giant grapes.

The climbers

Common ivy

Bindweed

Orchid

The climbers

Poison ivy
Don't touch - you might get a rash!

Hop

Pea
Open the pod to find the peas.

Bitter gourd

Soya bean

The climbers

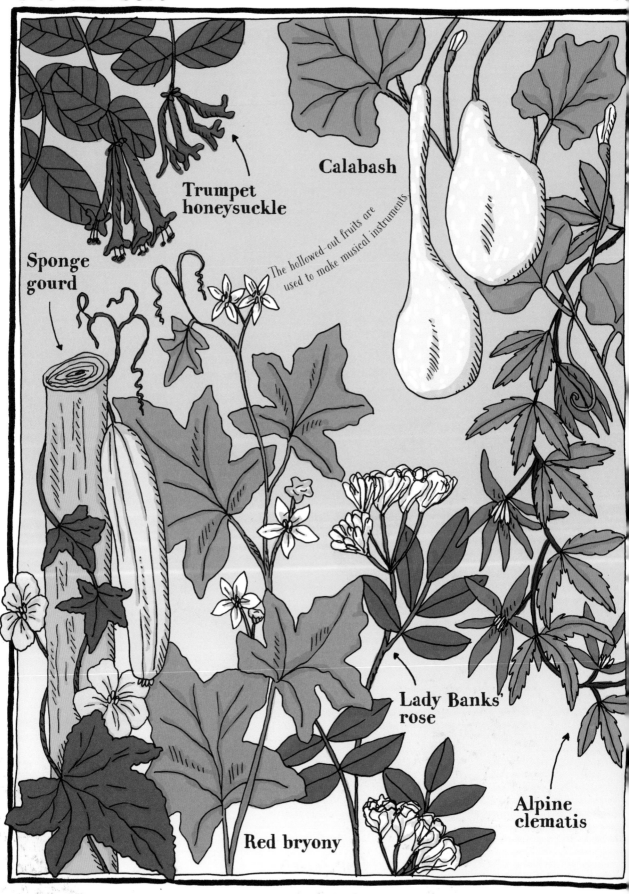

Trumpet
honeysuckle

Calabash

The hollowed-out fruits are used to make musical instruments

Sponge
gourd

Lady Banks'
rose

Alpine
clematis

Red bryony

The confused fruits

Fruits that think they're vegetables

Aubergine Aubergine contains seeds, which makes it a fruit.

Avocado The stone in the middle means that this is a fruit too.

Courgette Cut it open to see the seeds inside.

The confused fruits

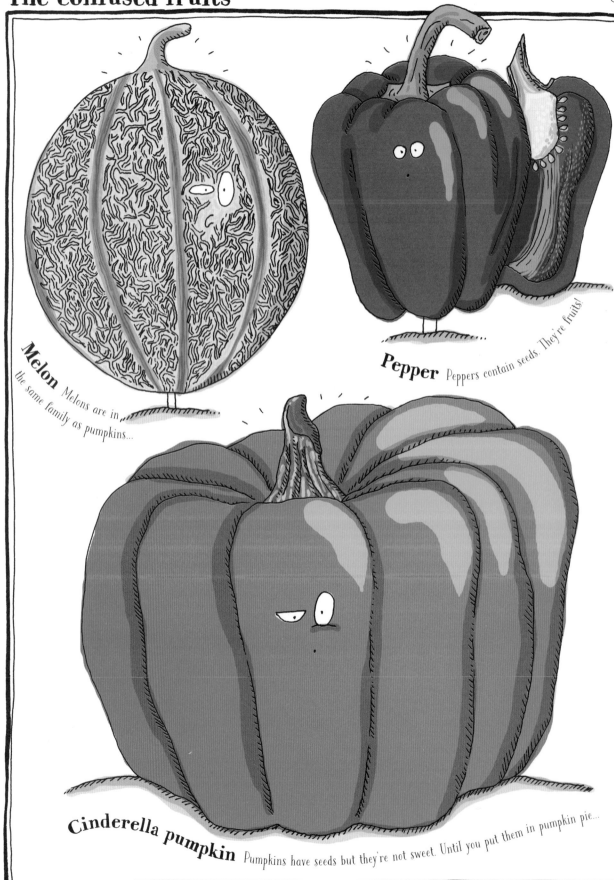

3

Melon Melons are in the same family as pumpkins...

Pepper Peppers contain seeds. They're fruits!

Cinderella pumpkin Pumpkins have seeds but they're not sweet. Until you put them in pumpkin pie...

Aladdin pumpkin Perfect for Halloween.

Gherkin A mini cucumber, usually pickled.

Vegetable pear Tastes like cucumber.

Tomato Comes in all shapes and sizes - but they're all fruits!

The deciduous trees

Trees with leaves that fall off in winter

Common lime tree

Crab apple An ancestor of the apples we eat every day.

Tulip tree
Tulip-like flowers grow on this tree in the spring and summer.

Shagbark hickory

Cherry elaeagnus

Aspen

Ash

Larch
Look out for
cones on the
ground in the
autumn.

Canadian sugar maple
The sweet sap in the trunk is used to make maple syrup.

Scarlet oak
The leaves turn a beautiful shade of red in autumn.

Rowan

The dyes

Indigo A dark-blue dye

Dyer's rocket
A yellow dye for silk and wool

The colour comes
from the leaves.

The whole plant
can be used to
make the dye.

The evergreens

Trees that stay green in winter

Umbrella pine *Pine nuts grow on this tree.*

Holm oak

Tasmanian snow gum
Related to the peppermint plant.

Australian banyan
Grows on the surface of another tree until its roots reach the ground. Then it strangles its host tree and takes over!

Strawberry tree The fruit looks like strawberries but tastes like figs.

Bay laurel The leaves are used to flavour stews.

Tea plant The leaves are dried to make tea.

Cape jasmine

The forest dwellers

Sweet cherry

Field elm

Euphorbia

Largeleaf linden

Guelder rose

Roble beech

Ash

Wild strawberry

Small cow-wheat

The forest dwellers

Old man's beard

Beech

Silver fir

Honeysuckle

Pincushion moss

Big shaggy-moss

The fruits you have to peel

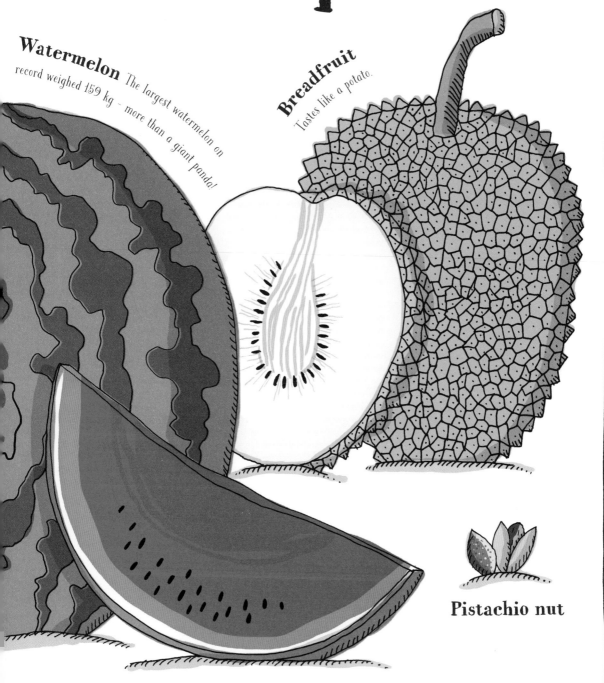

Watermelon *The largest watermelon on record weighed 159 kg - more than a giant panda!*

Breadfruit *Tastes like a potato.*

Pistachio nut

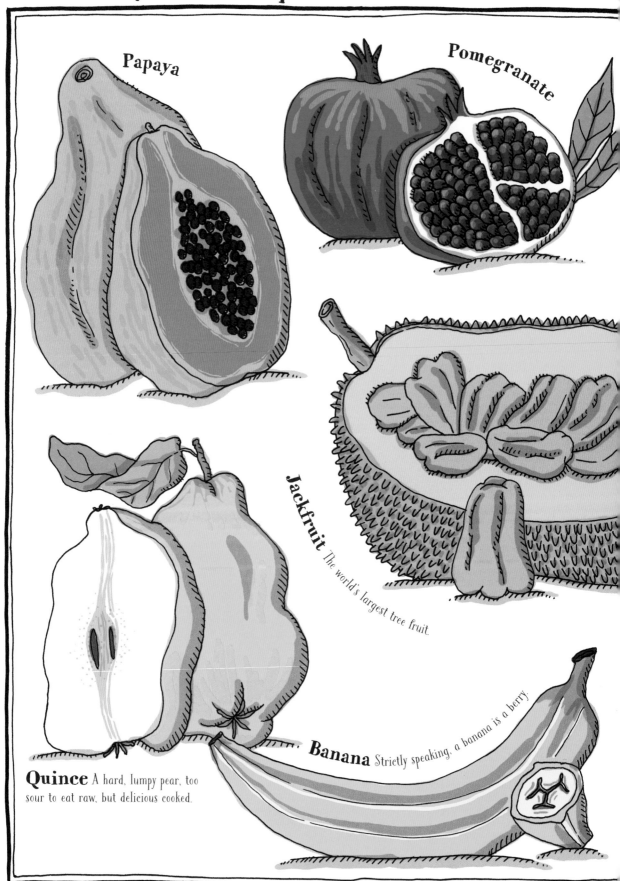

Papaya

Pomegranate

Jackfruit The world's largest tree fruit.

Quince A hard, lumpy pear, too sour to eat raw, but delicious cooked.

Banana Strictly speaking, a banana is a berry.

Passion fruit

Dragon fruit

Soursop Tastes like a cross between a pineapple and a strawberry.

Pineapple Pineapples were so rare and expensive in 16th-century Europe that wealthy people displayed them on dinner tables to show how much money they had spent on entertaining their guests.

The garden vegetables

Carrot

Potato

Skirret

Brussels sprout

Celery

Purple potato

Cabbage

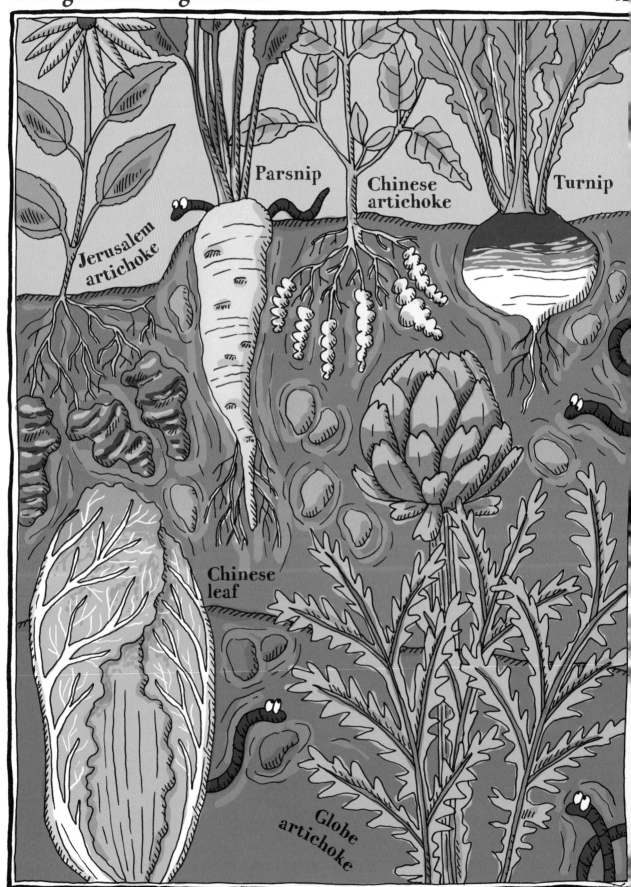

Jerusalem artichoke

Parsnip

Chinese artichoke

Turnip

Chinese leaf

Globe artichoke

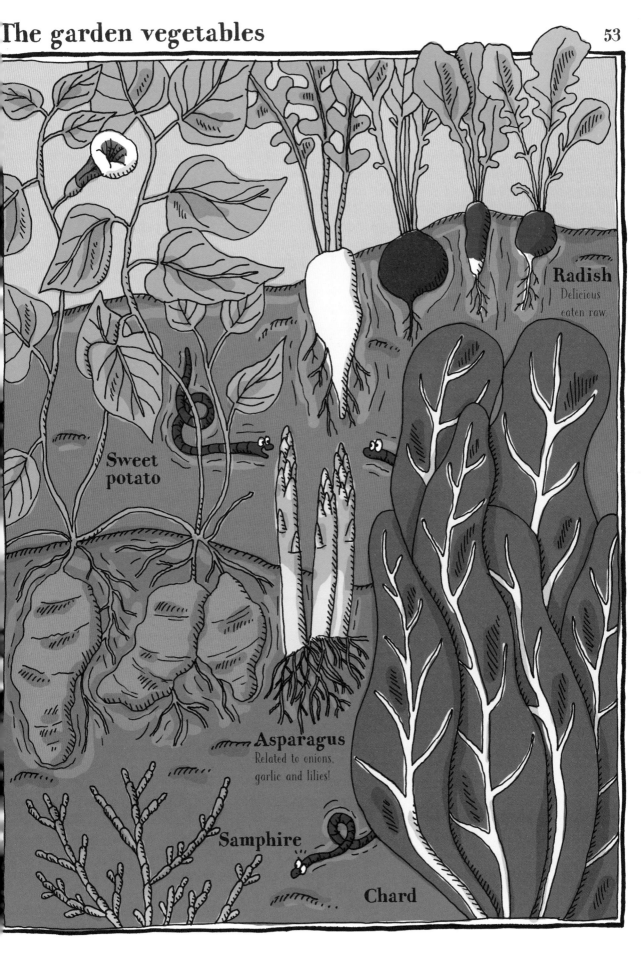

Radish
Delicious
eaten raw.

**Sweet
potato**

Asparagus
Related to onions,
garlic and lilies!

Samphire

Chard

The garden vegetables

Lentil
A good source
of protein.

Beetroot
The sweetest of all
vegetables. Beetroot is
very good for you,
but watch out ... the
juice can stain your
fingers pink!

Leek

Broccoli

Kohlrabi

Cucumber

Quinoa
Grown in South
America, this
healthy grain is
now popular all
over the world!

**Adzuki
beans**

Cauliflower

**Chinese
kale**

**Tuberous
chervil**

**Roman
cauliflower**

The giants

Titan arum
The flower smells like rotting meat and can grow to three metres tall – the height of a small tree.

The giants

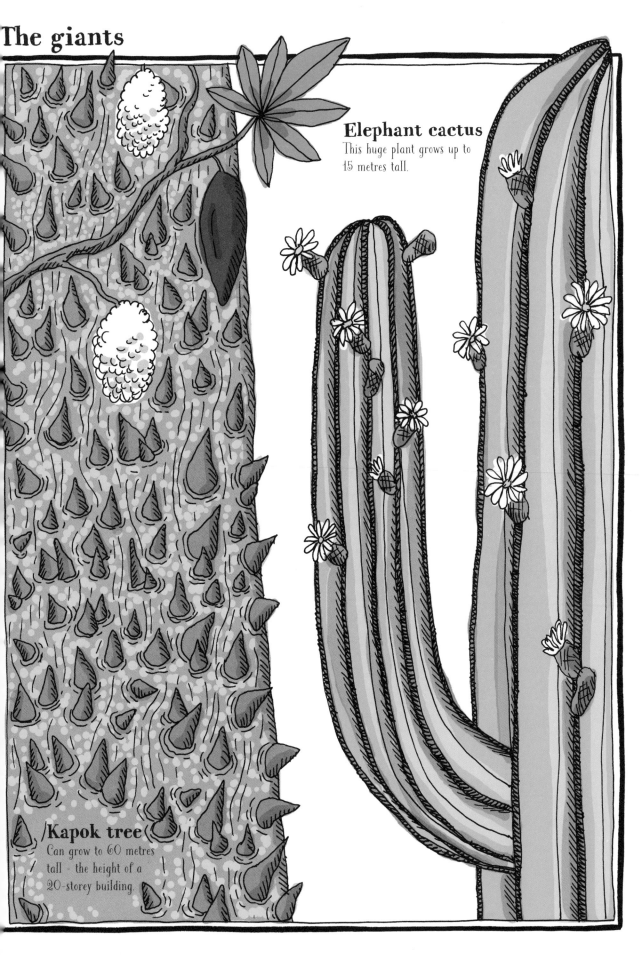

Elephant cactus
This huge plant grows up to
15 metres tall.

Kapok tree
Can grow to 60 metres
tall - the height of a
20-storey building.

Banyan tree
One tree is made up of lots
of trunks and it can spread
outwards for miles and miles.

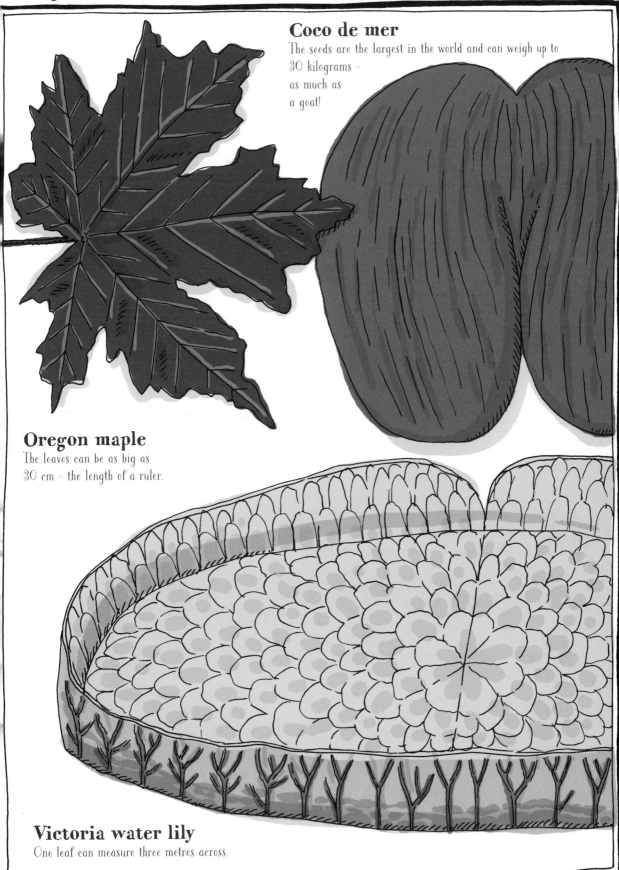

Coco de mer
The seeds are the largest in the world and can weigh up to 30 kilograms - as much as a goat!

Oregon maple
The leaves can be as big as 30 cm - the length of a ruler.

Victoria water lily
One leaf can measure three metres across.

Coast redwood
These trees can be over
110 metres tall.

The guests
Air plants and parasites

Mistletoe
Mistletoe is a parasite –
it sucks nutrients
from trees.

Giant philodendron
Air plants like this suck nutrients from the air.

Spanish moss
Air plant

Crocodile fern
Air plant

Ivy broomrape
Parasite

Strangling fig
Begins as an air plant but then
becomes a parasite.

Autograph tree
Air plant

Purple toothwort
Tree-root parasite

Orchid cactus
Air plant

White sandalwood
Parasite - gets nutrition from the roots of other trees.

Dodder
Parasite

Orchid
Air plant

Queen of the night
Air plant

The healers

Echinacea Strengthens the immune system.

Greater celandine For verrucas and warts.

Tea tree
An antiseptic.

Horehound
For digestive problems.

Male fern
Used to get rid of tapeworm –
a kind of worm that lives inside
an animal's body!

Chamomile Calms the nerves.

Wild mallow
Soothes coughs.

The healers

Quinine Protects against malaria and reduces fever.

Pink trumpet tree Antibacterial, and boots the immune system.

Pilewort Used to treat hemorrhoids.

Eyebright For eye infections.

Red vine leaf
Improves blood circulation.

Cypress tree
Helps wounds heal.

Liquorice
For stomach pain.

Yellow gentian
For stomach aches.

Scots pine Helps if you have a blocked-up nose.

Eucalyptus Antiseptic and good for the immune system.

Pepper Helps improve the digestion.

Common mallow Soothes the stomach.

Wild thyme Used to treat coughs and to help the digestion.

Lady's mantle Used as a painkiller and to heal wounds.

The herbs

Chives

The leaves taste a little like onion.

Common sage

Try this with chicken or pumpkin.

Every part of this plant is edible.

It tastes a bit like parsley.

Alexanders

Hyssop

Aniseed

Tastes like liquorice!

he herbs

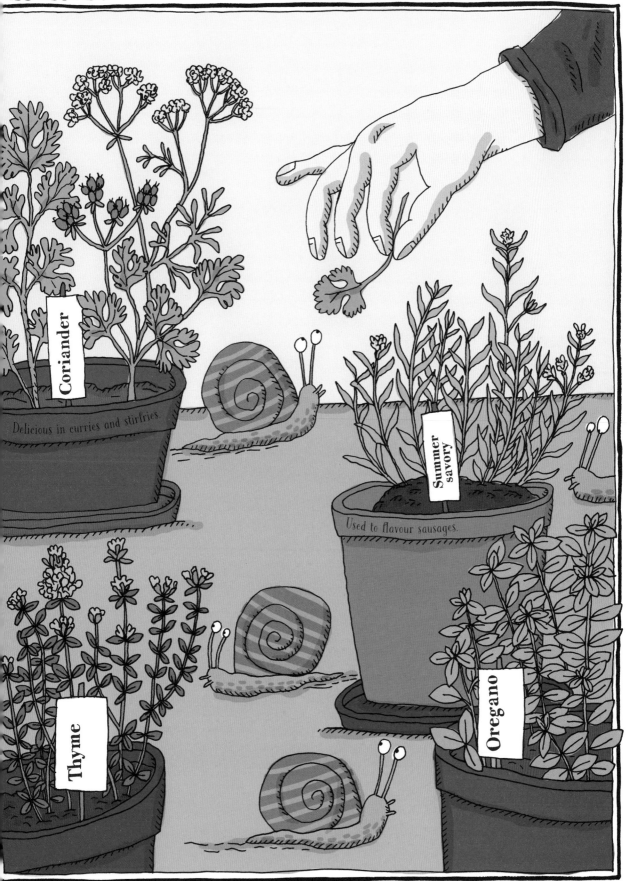

Coriander

Delicious in curries and stirfries.

Summer savory

Used to flavour sausages.

Thyme

Oregano

The herbs

Lovage

Tarragon

Parsley

Chew a sprig for fresh breath.

Verbena

Mint

Basil

Perfect for pasta and salads.

The historical

Mastic tree Its resin was used as chewing gum in ancient times.

Onion The people who built the pyramids were partly paid in onions.

Mastic tree resin

Bay laurel Ancient Greeks and Romans crowned brilliant poets, soldiers and sports people with laurel wreaths.

Canary Islands dragon tree
The red sap is known as dragon's blood. It was used as ink in Ancient Rome.

Chaste tree In the Middle Ages, monks used to eat the berries to stop them falling in love.

Camphor tree One of the first trees to grow back after a nuclear bomb was dropped on the Japanese city of Hiroshima on 6 August 1945.

Absinthe Used to make the spirit absinthe, which was popular in 19th-century France. The drink was banned for a while because drinking too much of it made people blind and mad.

Brown knapweed A Greek myth says this plant healed Chiron the centaur, after he was wounded by the god Hercules' arrow.

Poet's narcissus In Greek mythology, a hunter named Narcissus killed himself after falling hopelessly in love with his own reflection. The narcissus flower can often be found at the edge of lakes.

Hazel tree Witches were said to use hazel sticks to find water underground.

Houseleek Used to be planted on thatched roofs as people believed it protected houses from lightning strikes.

Azarole King Louis XIV of France loved eating azarole jam.

Resurrection plant This plant can survive for hundreds of years without water... when it rains, it springs back to life!

Valerian Has been used for centuries as a treat for cats - they love the smell.

Wet

Dry

The homebodies

Plants that only grow in one place

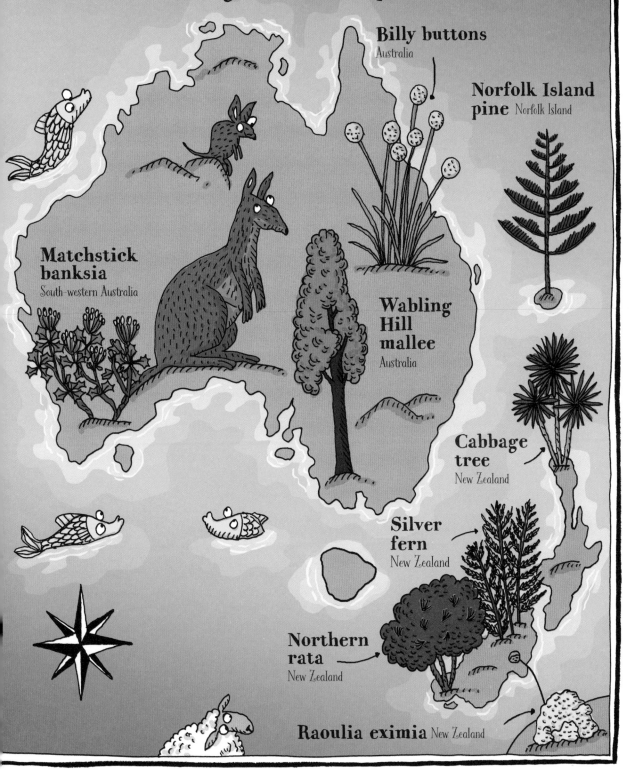

Billy buttons Australia

Norfolk Island pine Norfolk Island

Matchstick banksia South-western Australia

Wabling Hill mallee Australia

Cabbage tree New Zealand

Silver fern New Zealand

Northern rata New Zealand

Raoulia eximia New Zealand

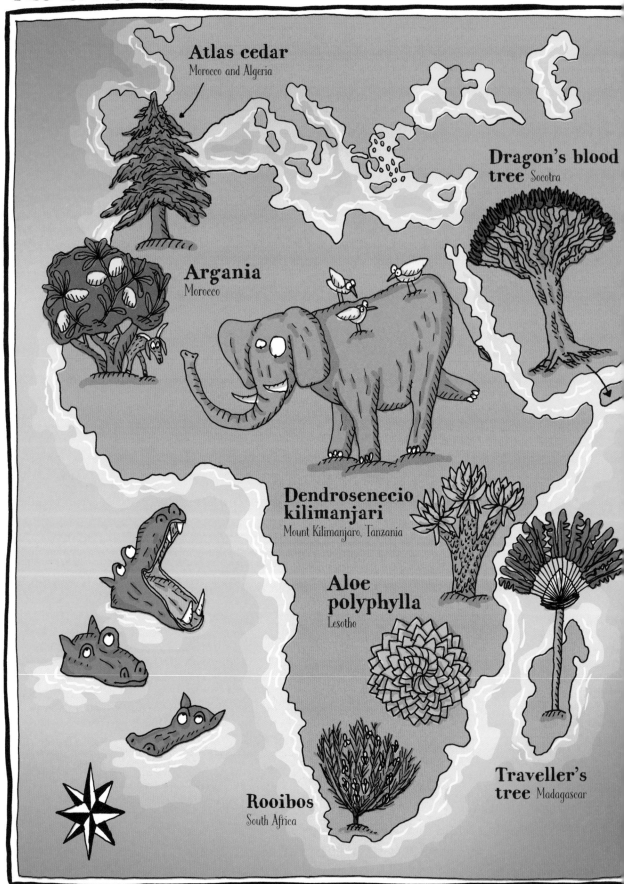

Atlas cedar
Morocco and Algeria

Dragon's blood tree Socotra

Argania
Morocco

Dendrosenecio kilimanjari
Mount Kilimanjaro, Tanzania

Aloe polyphylla
Lesotho

Rooibos
South Africa

Traveller's tree Madagascar

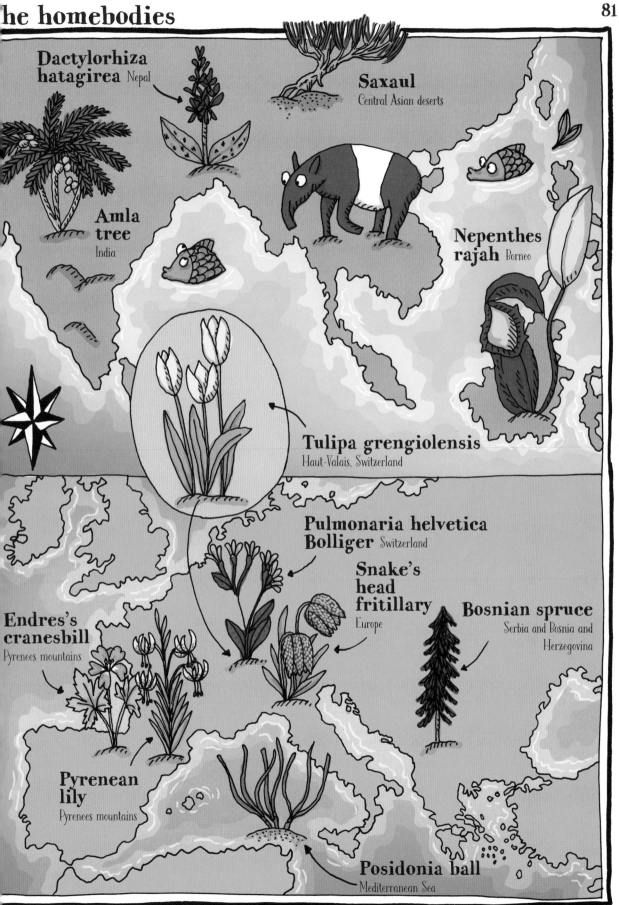

Dactylorhiza hatagirea Nepal

Saxaul
Central Asian deserts

Amla tree
India

Nepenthes rajah Borneo

Tulipa grengiolensis
Haut-Valais, Switzerland

Pulmonaria helvetica Bolliger Switzerland

Snake's head fritillary
Europe

Bosnian spruce
Serbia and Bosnia and Herzegovina

Endres's cranesbill
Pyrenees mountains

Pyrenean lily
Pyrenees mountains

Posidonia ball
Mediterranean Sea

Clay phacelia
Utah, USA

Sassafras
Forests in the eastern USA

**Queen of
the Andes**
Andes mountains, Chile
and Argentina

Argylia radiata
Chile

The hybrids

London plane tree A cross between an American sycamore and an oriental plane tree.

Chinese Magnolia Created in 1820 by Étienne Soulange-Bodin. A cross between a tulip tree and a lily magnolia.

Red horse chestnut A cross between a horse chestnut and a red buckeye.

The hybrids

Broad-leaved whitebeam
A cross between a wild service tree and a whitebeam.

Hybrid strawberry tree
A cross between a strawberry tree and a Greek strawberry tree.

Mandarin orange tree
The botanist Louis Trabut and Brother Clément Rodier created this tree in 1892 by crossing a mandarin tree and an orange tree.

Bollwiller pear A cross between a pear tree and a whitebeam.

'La France' rose This cross between a Madam Victor Verdier rose and a Madam Brevy tea rose was created accidentally in 1867 by rose-grower Jean-Baptiste Guillot.

Jostaberry
A cross between a blackcurrant bush and a gooseberry bush.

The imposters

These poisonous plants look just like harmless ones... watch out!

Lily of the valley
Poisonous!

Bear's garlic

Lily of the valley leaves are poisonous... but they look just like bear's garlic leaves.
If you rub a leaf and it smells like garlic, it's bear's garlic, so you're safe.

Poison hemlock
Very poisonous!

Queen Anne's lace

Chervil

These plants all look alike... so how can you tell the difference?
Crumple a leaf. If it's hemlock, the leaf will smell revolting, like urine.

Herb Paris
Poisonous!

Blueberry

Blueberries are delicious, but herb Paris berries are deadly.
Look at the leaves - blueberry leaves are much smaller.

Peruvian groundcherry

Shoo-fly plant
Poisonous!

The shoo-fly plant looks similar to the Peruvian groundcherry,
but its flowers are a different colour.

The lookalikes

Ginseng root Looks like a person.

Monkey orchid Smells like an orange. Looks like a happy monkey.

The lookalikes

Parrot balsam

Darth Vader plant The Force is strong in this one.

Dove orchid

Flying duck orchid

Naked man orchid

White egret flower

Impatiens bequaertii
Looks like a dancing girl.

Hot lips

The magical

Mandrake Used for both black and white magic as a powerful love potion. Some people used to think it was an animal rather than a plant.

The root looks like a human body.

Opium poppy
Black magic. Used in spells to make people fall asleep.

Love lies bleeding
White magic. Thought to make you invisible.

Caraway White magic. Used in love potions... and for taming pigeons!

Lily White magic. Carry a bulb around your neck to break a love spell.

Jimsonweed Black magic. Used in potions to cause hallucinations or sleep. Also called devil's snare.

Wild lettuce Black magic. Used as an ointment by witches to bring on hallucinations and sleep.

Darnel Black magic. This plant is said to be the devil's favourite and is used in witches' brews to cause blindness.

The meadow flowers

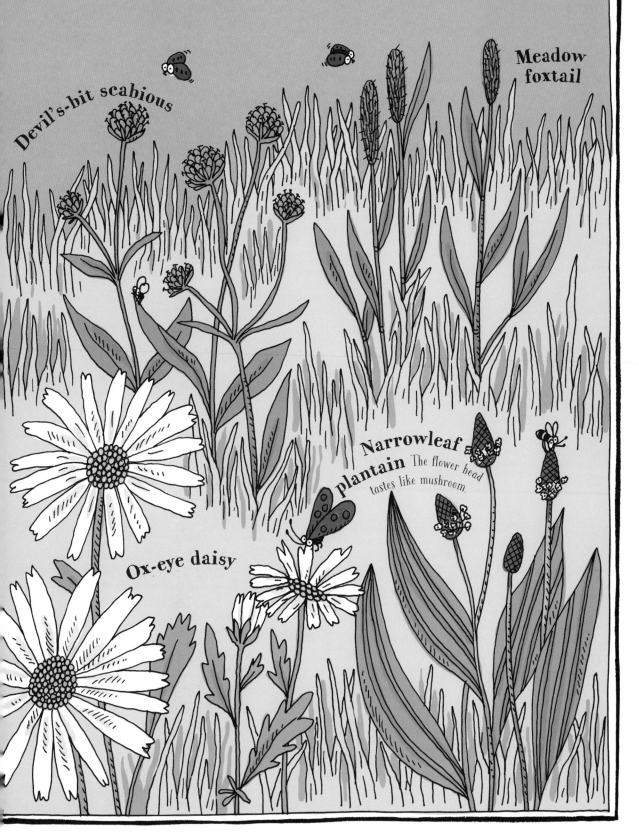

Devil's-bit scabious

Meadow foxtail

Narrowleaf plantain The flower head tastes like mushroom.

Ox-eye daisy

The meadow flowers

Cuckoo flower
This flowers around the time that cuckoos appear in spring.

Common verbena

Common Centaury
Used as a herbal tea.

Field pansy

Creeping buttercup

Adder's tongue

Field scabious

Spring crocus

Common daisy
Named 'day's eye' because
the flowers close
at night.

The meadow flowers

Quaking grass
Look out for it shaking in the breeze.

Round-headed rampion

Black medic

Autumn crocus

The mountaineers

Creeping avens

Windmill palm

Norway
spruce
Also known as the
Christmas tree!

Mountain
cornflower

Runner
bean

The mountaineers

Mountain pine

Rhododendron

Red fir
Older trees have
redder bark.

Bearberry

Spring
gentian

Narcissus
anemone

Monkey puzzle

Oriental beech

Himalayan birch

English lavender

Mountain avens

Common juniper

Giant sequoia
May live for over 3,000 years.

Ginkgo
Ginkgo trees have existed on Earth
for more than 270 million years.

Welwitschia mirabilis
Can live to be over 2,000 years old.

Sacred fig Can live for over 2,000 years.

Yew Can live for up to 5,000 years.

Small-leaved lime
Lives 500-1,000 years.

Douglas fir Lives for up to 6,000 years.

English oak
Lives for up to 1,000 years.

The ornamentals

Pretty plants

Chinese lantern In the spring, the lanterns dry up and you can see the fruit inside.

Trumpet vine

Japanese camellia

Japanese maple

The ornamentals

Weeping
pear

Silk tree

Canary Island date palm

Aloe yucca

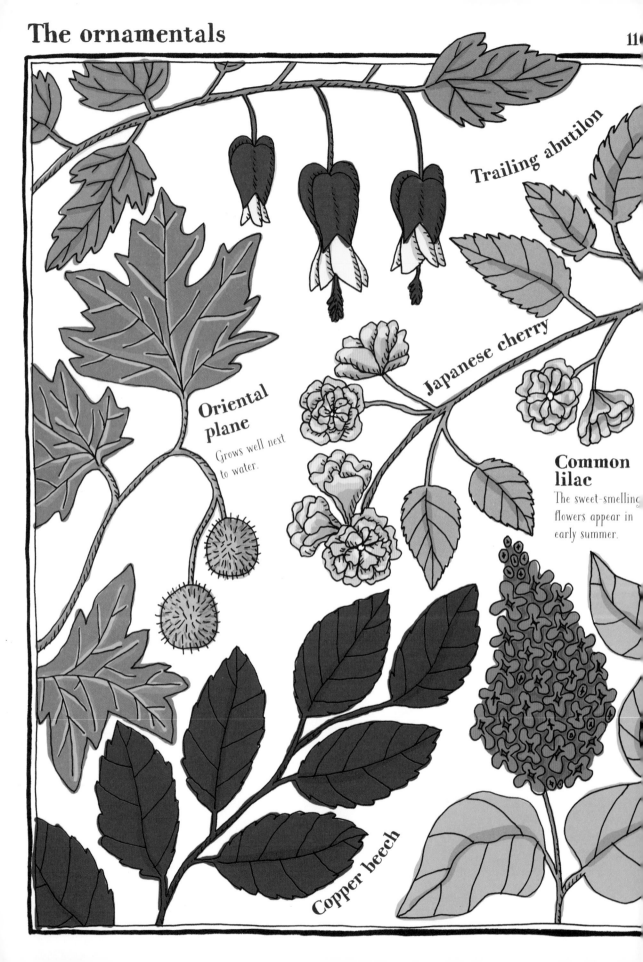

The ornamentals

Trailing abutilon

Japanese cherry

Oriental plane

Grows well next to water.

Common lilac

The sweet-smelling flowers appear in early summer.

Copper beech

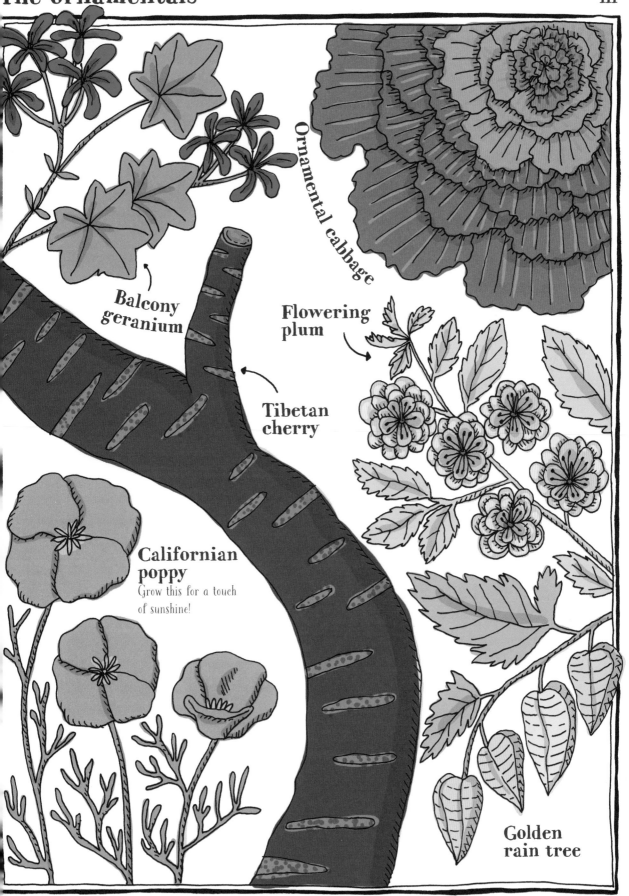

Balcony geranium

Ornamental cabbage

Flowering plum

Tibetan cherry

Californian poppy
Grow this for a touch of sunshine!

Golden rain tree

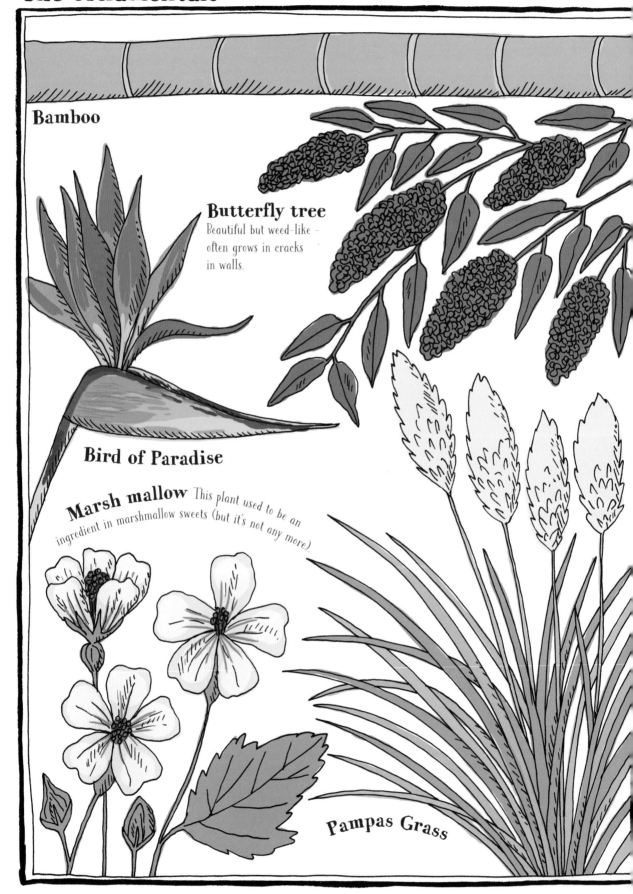

Bamboo

Butterfly tree
Beautiful but weed-like -
often grows in cracks
in walls.

Bird of Paradise

Marsh mallow This plant used to be an
ingredient in marshmallow sweets (but it's not any more).

Pampas Grass

The perennials

Plants that live for years and years!

Hyacinth
Smells sweet in the spring.

Musk mallow

Cowslip

Perennial ryegrass
The tough grass used for lawns and sports pitches.

Ground ivy Look out for it in woods and hedgerows.

Forget-me-not

Common rockrose

Marsh grass

Wild marjoram
Butterflies and bees love this plant.

Silverweed cinquefoil
Put a leaf in each shoe to get rid of sweaty feet!

Hydrangea

Sea kale

The perfumed

Clematis armandii

Grand fir The leaves give off the scent of mandarins when they're crushed.

Jasmine

Caramel tree Smells of caramel in the autumn.

Flowering ash Smells sweet. The sugary sap was once used as a sweetener, like maple syrup.

Garden mignonette

Mock orange

Wisteria

Cananga tree Ylang-ylang perfume comes from this tree.

Black locust tree

Moschatel Handle with care - the musky scent fades if the plant is bruised.

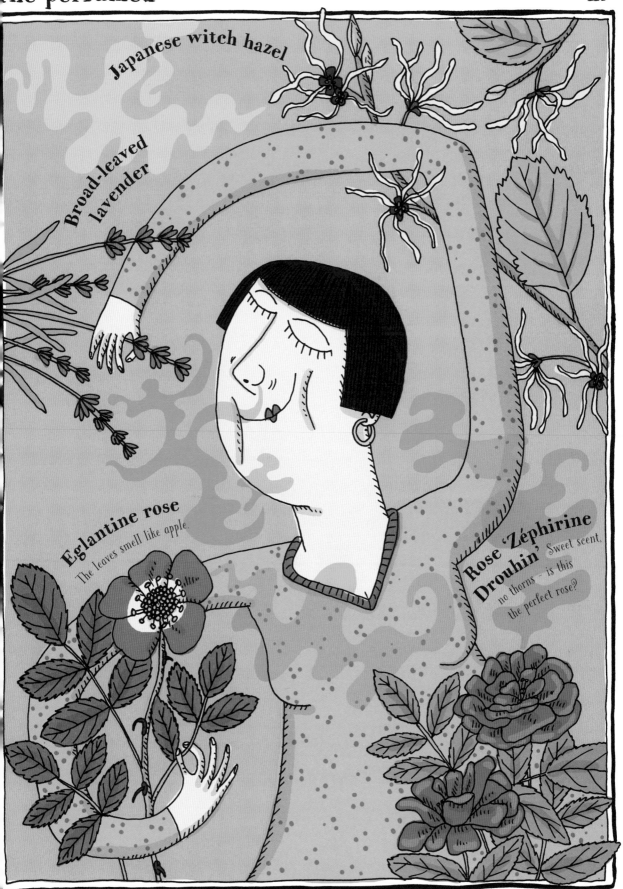

Japanese witch hazel

Broad-leaved lavender

Eglantine rose
The leaves smell like apple.

Rose 'Zéphirine Drouhin' Sweet scent, no thorns – is this the perfect rose?

The poisoners

Solomon's seal *The berry is deadly*

Deadly nightshade *The berry and root are poisonous*

English monkshood
The leaf and root could kill you!

Red angel trumpet
Avoid the whole plant if you want to stay alive!

February daphne
Even touching this plant could bring you out in a rash.

Rue
Avoid the leaves!

Climbing onion
The bulbs look like onions, but don't eat them!

The poisoners

Giant fennel
This plant is related to the carrot -
but don't be fooled into taking a bite!

Oleander
The whole plant is
poisonous...

Henbane
'Hen' means 'death'...

Sun spurge
Will make you very sick!

Feverfew
The leaves are used
to treat headaches...
but too much can be
toxic!

The poisoners

Manchineel tree
One of the most poisonous trees - don't shelter under it if it's raining!

Manchineel sap burns the skin!

Strychnine tree
In the 19th century, poison from this tree was used to murder people...

Devil's trumpet
One of the world's most deadly plants. Even smelling the flowers can harm you!

Birthwort
This plant is still used in herbal medicine - but watch out, it could kill you!

Poisonberry
The fruit is poisonous.

The prickly

Prickly pear

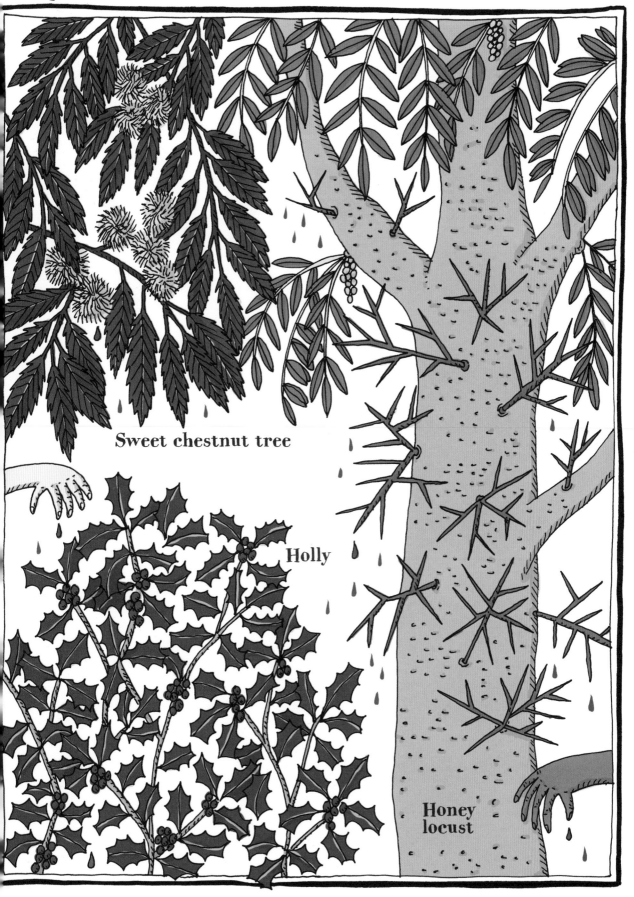

Sweet chestnut tree

Holly

Honey locust

The prickly

Barberry The berries are full of vitamin C.

Hawthorn

Beach rose

Artichoke thistle

Japanese bitter orange

Anchor plant

Rat tail cactus

A trailing plant to grow indoors.

Gorse

Dog rose

Common thistle

The prickly

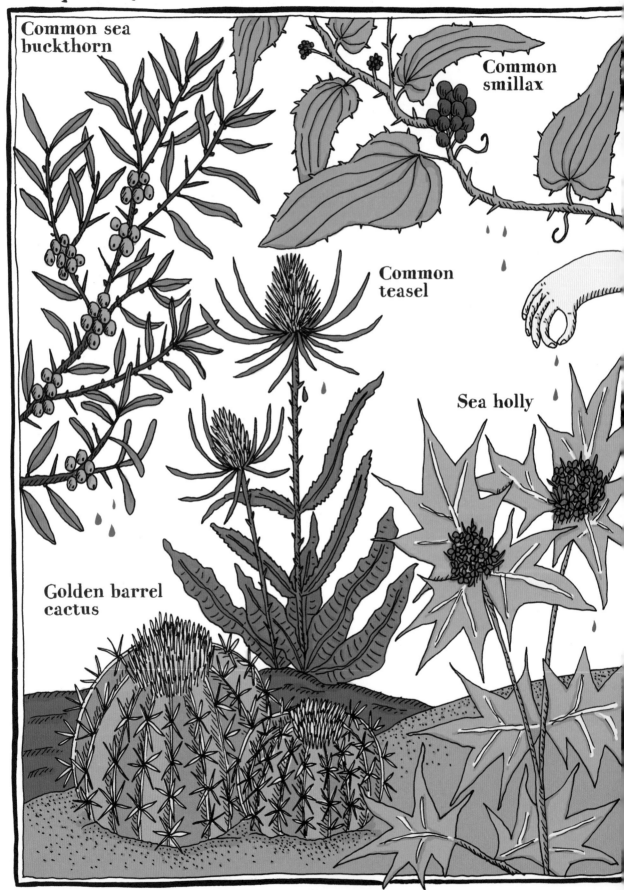

Common sea buckthorn

Common smillax

Common teasel

Sea holly

Golden barrel cactus

The reds and pinks

Gallic rose The ancestor of many garden rose varieties.

Pink sorrel

Red alder The bark turns red when it's damaged.

Bougainvillea

Great willowherb

Hardy fuchsia

Sargent's cherry

New Zealand
Christmas tree

Ragged
robin

Japanese maple The Japanese name 'kito' means 'calm' or 'at peace'

Common poppy Symbol of wartime remembrance.

Lipstick tree

Hoary rock-rose

Tuberous pea

Hollyhock This cottage garden flower can grow to over 2.5 metres tall!

Restharrow

Common vetch

The rock plants

Edelweiss
Edelweiss leaves look woolly because they're covered in hairs that protect it from the cold.

The rock plants

Whitebeam

The wood can be used to make furniture.

Staghorn sumac

Caper

Caper berries are delicious pickled.

Anthyllis barba-jovis

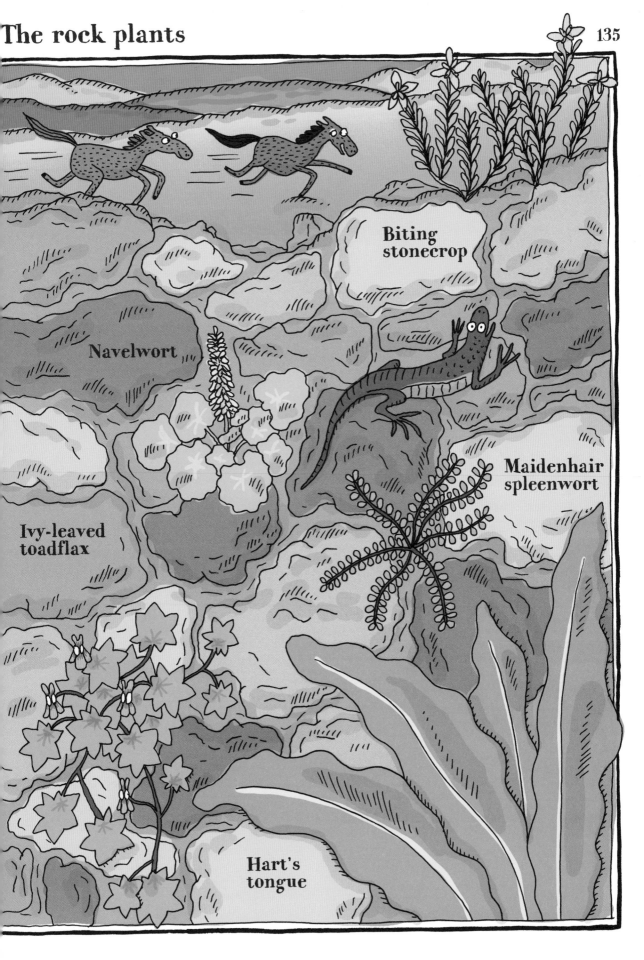

Biting
stonecrop

Navelwort

Ivy-leaved
toadflax

Maidenhair
spleenwort

Hart's
tongue

The rock plants

European fan palm

Elephant's trunk
Watch out for the spikes on the trunk!

Frankincense

Alpine aster

Wild tulip

Judas tree

Salad burnet

Upright
brome

Stemless
carline
thistle

Bladder
campion

Bird's-foot
trefoil

The salads

Round lettuce Perfect in a cheese sandwich.

Garden cress Tastes peppery.

Winter purslane

Red leaf lettuce

Batavia lettuce

Spinach *Packed with vitamins and iron*

Belgian endive
Grows best in the dark!

Verona red chicory

Rocket Salad with a peppery kick

Lamb's lettuce

Nasturtium The flowers are edible!

The sand lovers

Joshua tree Mainly grows in the Mojave desert in the USA.

Horsetail

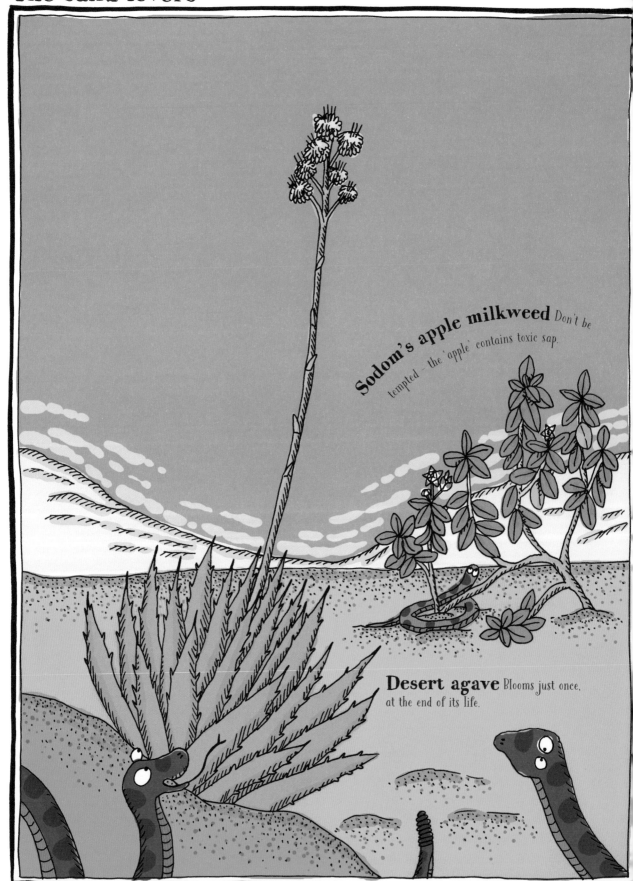

Sodom's apple milkweed Don't be tempted – the 'apple' contains toxic sap.

Desert agave Blooms just once, at the end of its life.

Saguaro cactus An icon of America's Wild West.

Aloe vera The sap comes in handy for soothing sunburn.

Creosote bush

Silver birch The wind-blown seeds of this tree are often the first to sprout on empty ground

Caucasian elm

California tree poppy

Carthusian pink

The sand lovers

Maritime pine

Sea stock Often the first plant you'll see at the top of a beach.

The seed sowers

Touch-me-not
When the fruit is touched, it spits out its seeds.

Burdock The seeds have little hooks that attach themselves to the coats of passing animals.

Hogweed The seeds are spread by the wind.

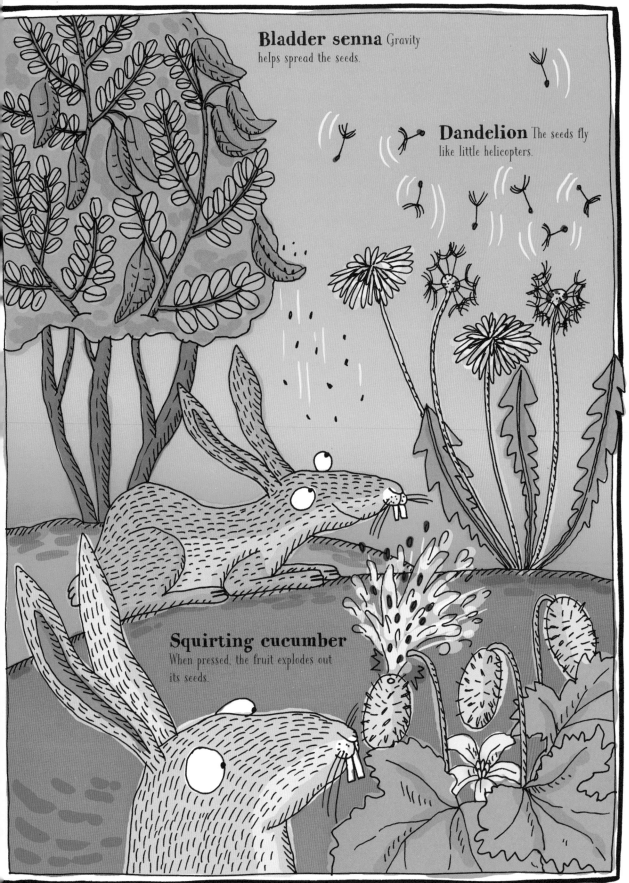

Bladder senna Gravity helps spread the seeds.

Dandelion The seeds fly like little helicopters.

Squirting cucumber When pressed, the fruit explodes out its seeds.

Coconut tree The fruit falls into the water and floats until it reaches the bank.

Sycamore maple The seeds have wings!

Black poplar If you see something that looks like cotton wool floating in the air, it's probably poplar seeds.

The spices

Dill seed
Delicious in stews.

Timur pepper
Tangy and hot, great with fish.

Turmeric Brings warmth and colour to curries.

Cubeb pepper

Cumin Has been popular for 2,000 years.

Wasabi Super spicy. Eat with sushi.

Vanilla The seed pod of an orchid plant.

White mustard Great for making pickles.

Saffron The most expensive spice.

Cinnamon The bark of the cinnamon tree. Delicious in cakes and biscuits.

Horseradish Hot and zingy!

Black pepper Peppercorns are tiny dried fruits.

Cloves Tiny dried flower buds, great with meat or fruit.

Cardamom Spicy-sweet, ideal for curries.

The spotty and stripy

Malabar gourd Sailors on long voyages used to eat these because they stay fresh for a year.

Zebra plant

Never-never plant

Ivy-leaved cyclamen

Monkey flower

Lungwort The leaves look like lungs

Tiger lily

Dumb cane

Marsh orchid

Spotted medick

Yellow
woodsorrel

Wood
anemone

Bank moss

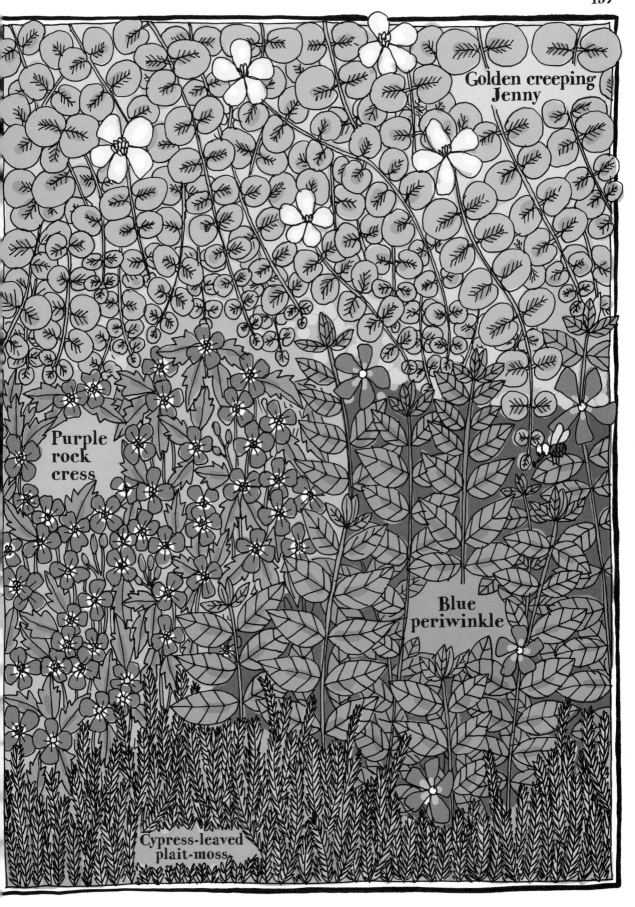

Golden creeping
Jenny

Purple
rock
cress

Blue
periwinkle

Cypress-leaved
plait-moss,

The stars

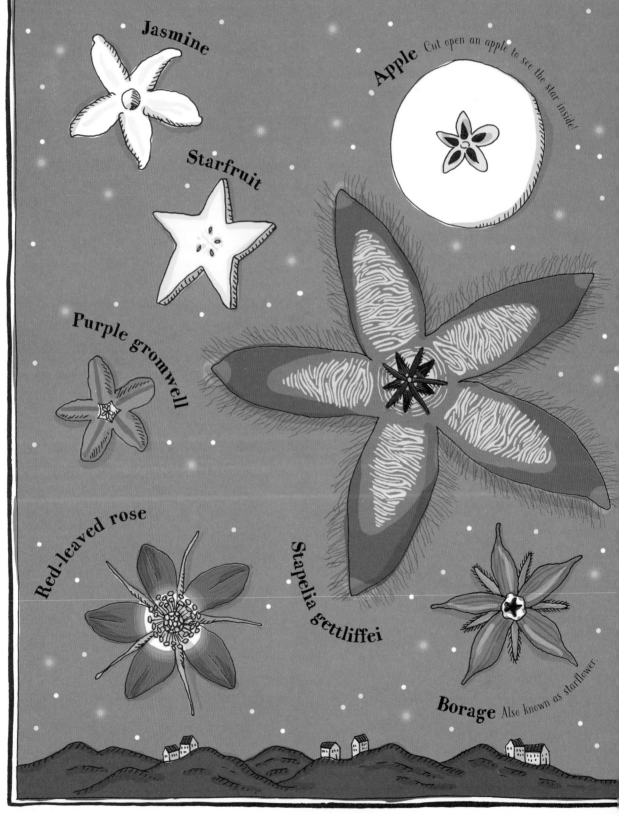

Jasmine

Apple Cut open an apple to see the star inside!

Starfruit

Purple gromwell

Red-leaved rose

Stapelia gettliffei

Borage Also known as starflower

The stars

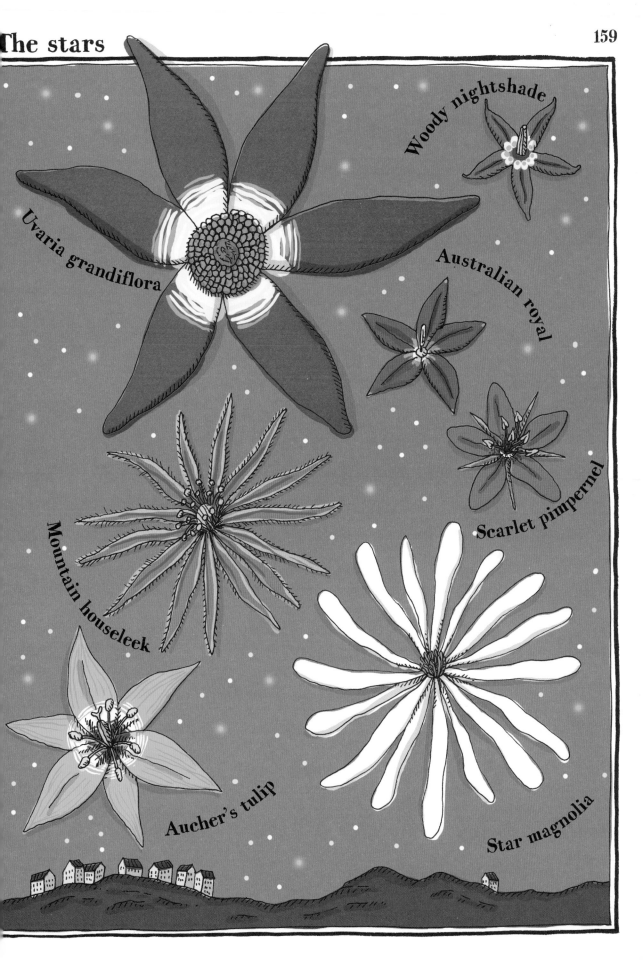

Woody nightshade

Uvaria grandiflora

Australian royal

Scarlet pimpernel

Mountain houseleek

Aucher's tulip

Star magnolia

Spiderwort

White hellebore

Castor oil plant

Snow gentian

Branched asphodel

Star anise

The stinkers

Stinking corpse lily A parasite on other plants.
The stench attracts flies, which then pollinate it.

The stinkers

Tree of Heaven Badly named, unless your idea of heaven is the smell of sweaty socks.

Durian Banned from public places in Southeast Asia because of its smell, but it tastes delicious.

Jackal food plant Smells like poo.

Stinking gum Used as a spice. When cooked, it stops stinking and starts to smell like leeks.

Lords-and-ladies Gives off heat to make its dung scent more attractive to flies

The stoned fruits

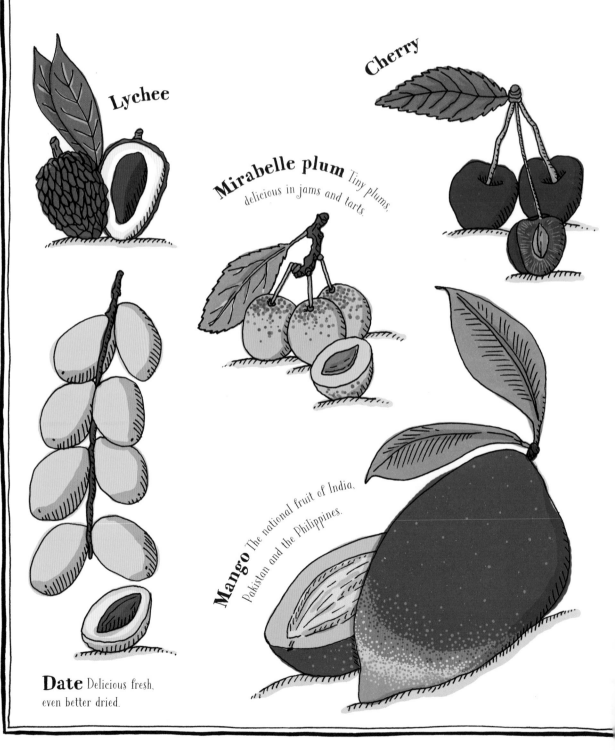

Lychee

Cherry

Mirabelle plum *Tiny plums, delicious in jams and tarts.*

Mango *The national fruit of India, Pakistan and the Philippines.*

Date Delicious fresh, even better dried.

Nectarine

Apricot *People have been growing apricots for 5,000 years.*

Greengage *Small, round and super sweet.*

Damson

Peach

Victoria plum

Loquat

The tasty fruits

Blackberry

Barbados cherry

Pear

Raspberry

Strawberry

Fig Figs are actually inside-out flowers.

Persimmon Delicious fresh, cooked or dried.

Kiwi fruit Contains five times as much vitamin C as an orange.

Currant

Serviceberry

Cashew nut The 'nut' is a seed that grows at the tip of the cashew apple.

Hardy kiwi These look like kiwis, but you don't need to peel them.

Goji berry

The transformers

Goosegrass The roasted seeds can be used as an alternative to coffee.

Stevia The leaves are used to sweeten food.

Black locust
Bees turn the pollen of this flower into the most delicious honey.

Carob tree
Used to make carob, a substitute for chocolate.

Swiss chard
The roots can be made into sugar.

Drumstick tree The leaves are used to make moringa, which is delicious sprinkled on soup.

Chicory The root can be roasted and ground to make a kind of coffee.

Cocoa tree Chocolate is made from the beans!

Rambutan

African tulip tree

Rainbow gum

Arabica coffee

Silver brake fern

Silk cotton tree

Red mangrove

Screwpine The leaves are used to make bags, boxes and furniture.

Spanish cane

Coca

Brazil nut *Cut open the fruit to find the nuts.*

Royal poinciana

Sensitive plant *The leaves curl when touched, but then reopen.*

Pink quill

The useful

Flax The plant is used to make clothes, and the oil is used as a varnish and to make ink.

Hemp Used to make clothes and to insulate houses.

Caper spurge
Repels moles!

Neem tree
Kills insects.

NEEM OIL

Cotton Used to make all sorts of clothes.

Spindle tree The branches are burned to make charcoal.

Broom Dried branches are used to make brooms.

Rubber tree The sap of the tree is used to make rubber.

Common osier
Used to make baskets.

Walnut The shells are used to colour wood.

Walnut furniture dye

Chinese lacquer tree The poisonous sap is used as a lacquer in Asia to add shine to furniture and other objects.

The whites and yellows

Turkestan tulip

Coltsfoot
*Named after its
horse-shoe-shaped leaves.*

Primrose
*When you see a primrose,
you know that spring
has arrived.*

The whites and yellows

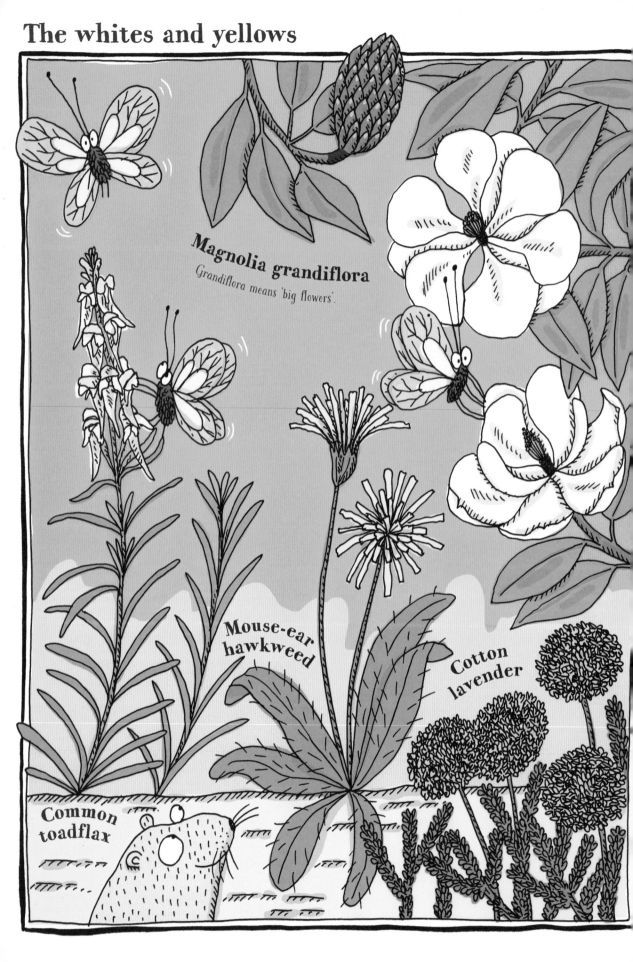

Magnolia grandiflora

Grandiflora means 'big flowers'.

Mouse-ear
hawkweed

Cotton
lavender

Common
toadflax

Birch

Pacific dogwood

Forsythia

Butternut squash

Yellow foxglove

Dewberry

Golden rod

Fringed water lily

Common wallflower

Snowdrop tree

Spiraea x vanhouttei

Field buttercup

Yellow rocket
Farmers love this because its leaves are poisonous to insects.

Sunflower

White campion

Handkerchief
tree

Sunflower seeds
make a tasty snack.

Daffodil

Corn chamomile

Groundsel

Fennel

Curry plant

**Evening
primrose**

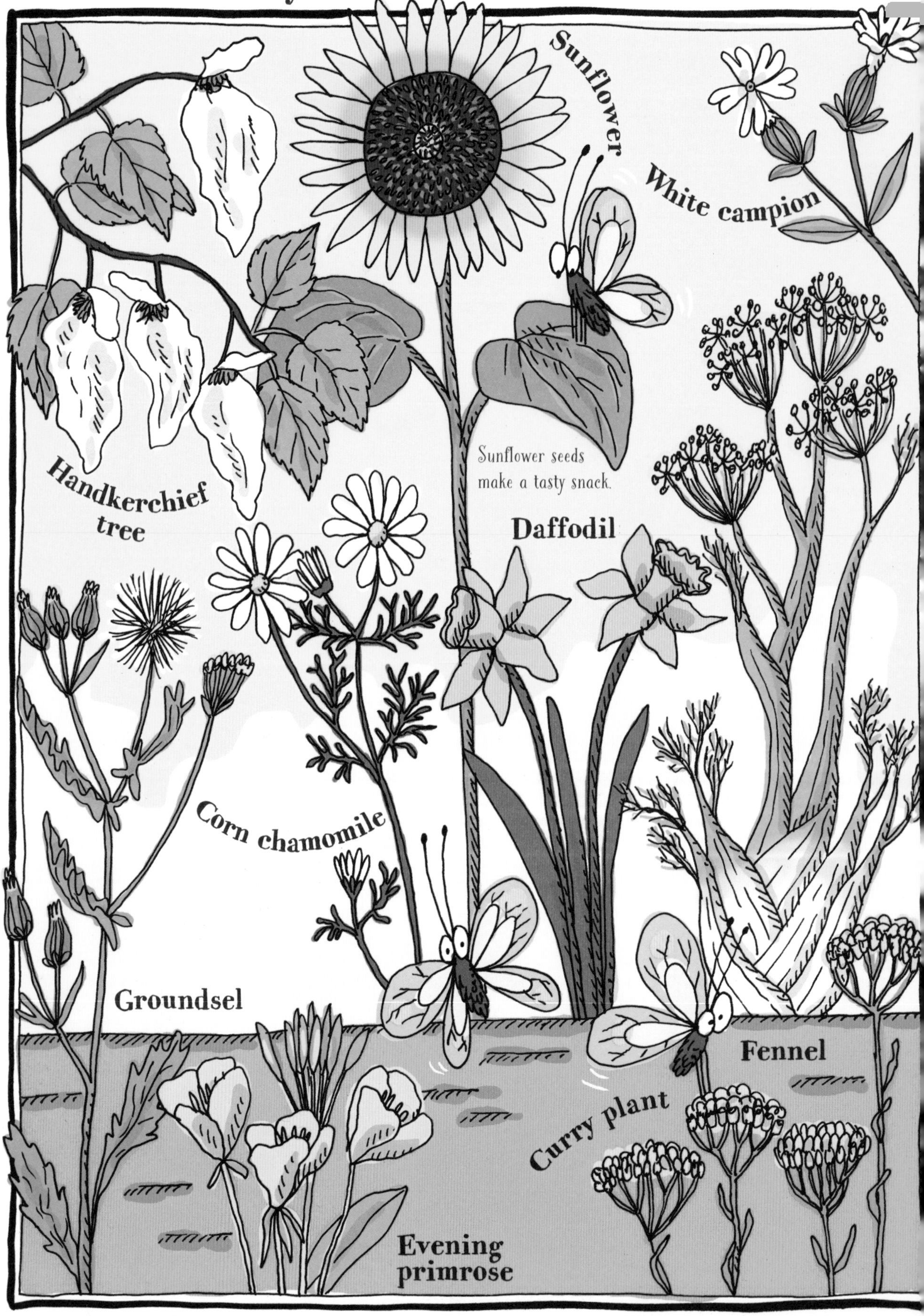

Appendix: leaf shapes

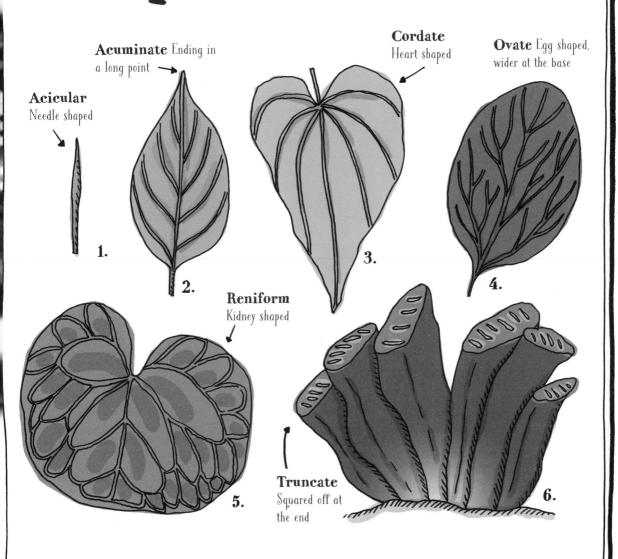

Acicular Needle shaped

Acuminate Ending in a long point

Cordate Heart shaped

Ovate Egg shaped, wider at the base

1.

2.

3.

4.

Reniform Kidney shaped

5.

Truncate Squared off at the end

6.

1. Blue spruce

2. Male dogwood

3. Black bryony

4. Snowberry

5. European wild ginger

6. Horse's teeth

Leaf shapes

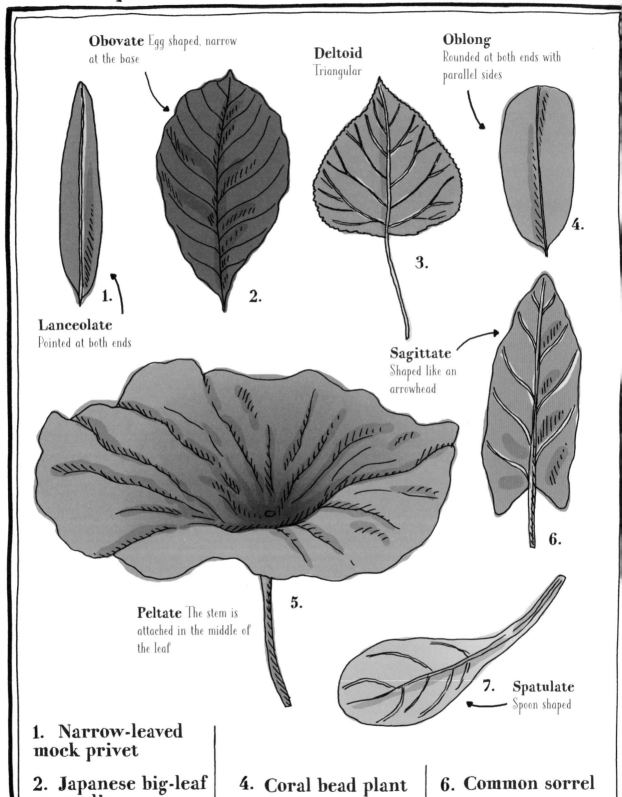

Obovate Egg shaped, narrow at the base

Deltoid Triangular

Oblong Rounded at both ends with parallel sides

1.

2.

3.

4.

Lanceolate Pointed at both ends

Sagittate Shaped like an arrowhead

6.

Peltate The stem is attached in the middle of the leaf

5.

7. **Spatulate** Spoon shaped

1. **Narrow-leaved mock privet**

2. **Japanese big-leaf magnolia**

3. **Black poplar**

4. **Coral bead plant**

5. **Sacred lotus**

6. **Common sorrel**

7. **Lamb's lettuce**

Leaf arrangement

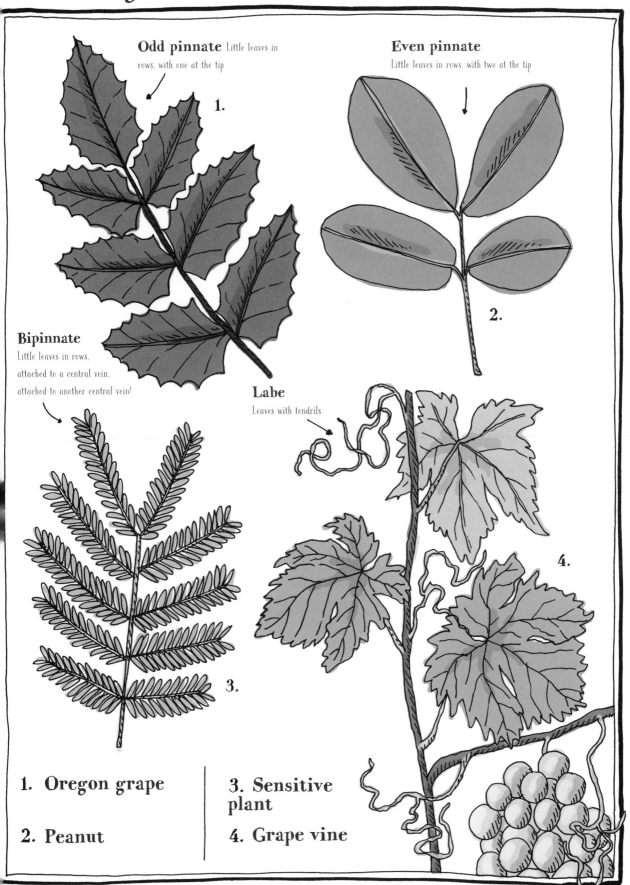

Odd pinnate Little leaves in rows, with one at the tip

1.

Even pinnate Little leaves in rows, with two at the tip

2.

Bipinnate Little leaves in rows, attached to a central vein, attached to another central vein!

Labe Leaves with tendrils

3.

4.

1. Oregon grape

2. Peanut

3. Sensitive plant

4. Grape vine

Leaf arrangement

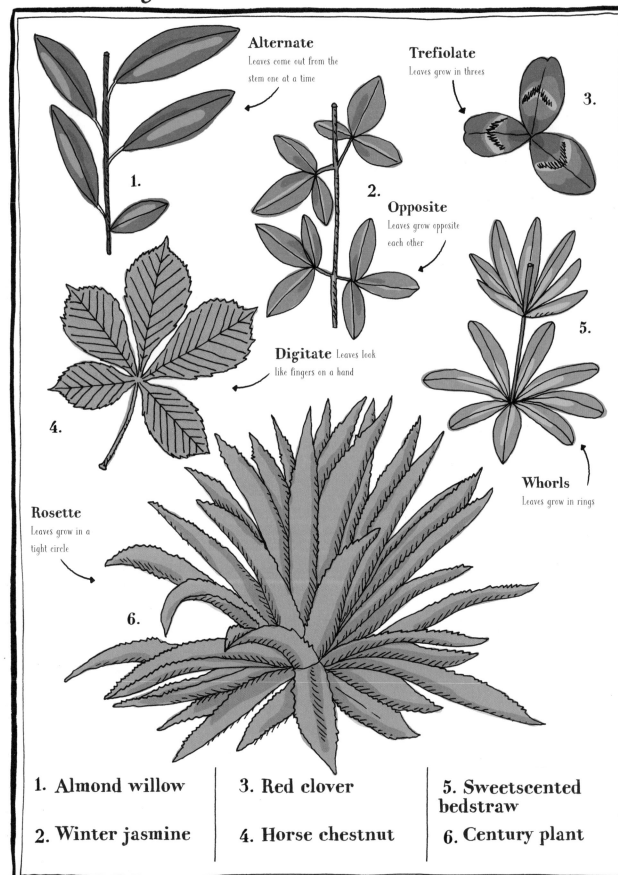

Alternate
Leaves come out from the stem one at a time

Trefiolate
Leaves grow in threes

3.

1.

2.

Opposite
Leaves grow opposite each other

5.

Digitate Leaves look like fingers on a hand

4.

Whorls
Leaves grow in rings

Rosette
Leaves grow in a tight circle

6.

1. Almond willow	3. Red clover	5. Sweetscented bedstraw
2. Winter jasmine	4. Horse chestnut	6. Century plant

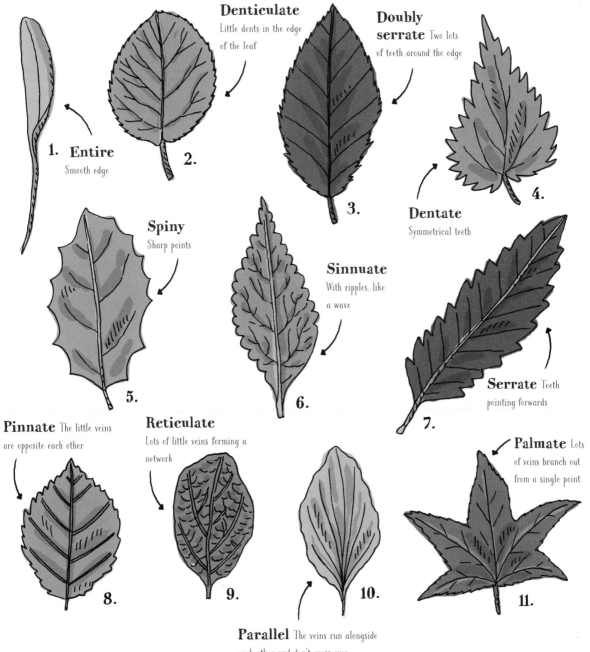

Denticulate Little dents in the edge of the leaf

Doubly serrate Two lots of teeth around the edge

1. **Entire** Smooth edge

2.

3.

4.

Dentate Symmetrical teeth

Spiny Sharp points

Sinnuate With ripples, like a wave

5.

6.

Serrate Teeth pointing forwards

7.

Pinnate The little veins are opposite each other

Reticulate Lots of little veins forming a network

Palmate Lots of veins branch out from a single point

8.

9.

10.

11.

Parallel The veins run alongside each other and don't cross over

1. **Sickle-leaved hare's ear**

2. **Viburnum**

3. **Common hornbeam**

4. **Nettle**

5. **Kermes oak**

6. **Dog's mercury**

7. **Chestnut oak**

8. **Dutch elm**

9. **Net-leaved willow**

10. **Broadleaf plantain**

11. **Sweet gum**

Glossary

Here are some words you might come across when you're reading about plants.

Air plant: A plant that absorbs water and nutrients from the atmosphere.

Annual: A plant that lives and dies over the course of a single year.

Aquatic plant: A plant that grows in water.

Biennial: A plant with a life cycle that takes place over two years. It usually flowers every other year.

Botany: The scientific study of plants.

Carnivorous plant: A plant that gets nutrients by trapping and consuming animals, usually insects.

Carpel: The female reproductive part of a flower.

Cereal: A grain (seed), such as wheat or barley, that is used for food.

Creeping: A plant that grows along the ground, producing roots along the way.

Deciduous: A tree or shrub that sheds its leaves every year.

Evergreen: A plant that keeps its leaves all year round.

Exotic: A plant that isn't originally from the place it's growing.

Flower: The part of a plant that produces seeds.

Fruit: The part of a plant that contains seeds.

Grain: The seed of a cereal plant, such as wheat.

Herb: The leaf of a plant used to flavour food.

Herbaceous: A plant that doesn't have woody stems that you can see above ground.

Horticulture: The art of growing plants.

Houseplant: A plant that is grown indoors.

Hybrid: A plant that is a cross between two different species or varieties.

Leaf: The part of a plant, growing out from a stem, that allows the plant to get energy from the sun.

Native: A plant that naturally grows in a certain place.

Ornamental: A plant grown because it is beautiful to look at.

Parasitic: A plant that gets its water and nutrients from another plant.

Petal: The segments around the stamen in a flower. They're usually coloured to attract pollinators such as bees.

Perennial: A plant that lives for more than two years.

Pollen: A powdery substance, released by the male reproductive part of a flower, that fertilizes the female part of a flower.

Pollination: The transfer of pollen from the male reproductive part of a flower to the female reproductive part of a flower.

Pollinator: An animal, such as a bee, that moves pollen from the male reproductive part of a flower to the female reproductive part of a plant, to fertilize it.

Root: The part of a plant that usually grows below the surface of the earth or water, that doesn't have any leaves on it.

Seed: The part of a plant that can reproduce, creating another plant.

Shrub: A woody plant that's smaller than a tree and has several stems at ground level.

Spice: The root, flower, bark or seed of a plant, used to flavour food.

Stamen: The male reproductive part of a flower, which produces pollen.`

Stem: The main body (or stalk) of a plant that usually grows up from the ground.

Tendril: Part of a climbing plant that attaches itself to support.

Thorn: A sharp, woody spike that sticks out of a plant to protect it from creatures that want to eat it.

Tree: A woody plant with one main stem (or trunk) growing up from the ground.

Tropical plant: A plant that grows naturally in the hot, wet climate of the equator, the imaginary ring around the centre of the Earth.

Vegetable: A plant (or part of a plant) that you eat.

Vein: A thin rib that runs through a leaf, giving the leaf structure and moving water around the leaf.

Woody: A plant, such as a tree or shrub, that produces wood to give itself structure.

Index

My warmest thanks to:
curator and ethnobotanist Didier Roguet, for his invaluable corrections;
Peggy Adam; Mirjana Farkas; Anne HB and Malizia Moulin for their help
in bringing certain families to life.

And also to Aldo, for his invaluable support, and to my family for their encouragement.

A·B·

Brimming with creative inspiration, how-to projects, and useful information to enrich your everyday life, Quarto Knows is a favourite destination for those pursuing their interests and passions. Visit our site and dig deeper with our books into your area of interest: Quarto Creates, Quarto Cooks, Quarto Homes, Quarto Lives, Quarto Drives, Quarto Explores, Quarto Gifts, or Quarto Kids.

Plantopedia © 2018 Éditions La Joie de Lire SA

Illustrated by Adrienne Barman
Designed by Pascale Rosier
Additional text and translation into English by Amy-Jane Beer and Felicity Davidson

First published in Switzerland in 2018 under the title *Drôle d'encyclopédie végétale* by Éditions La Joie de Lire SA, 5 Chemin Neuf, CH-1207 Genève, Switzerland

First published in the English language in 2018 by Wide Eyed Editions, an imprint of The Quarto Group.
The Old Brewery, 6 Blundell Street, London N7 9BH, United Kingdom.
T (0)20 7700 6700 F (0)20 7700 8066 **www.QuartoKnows.com**

A catalogue record for this book is available from the British Library.

ISBN 978-1-78603-138-9

The illustrations were created digitally
Set in Didodot and Bookeyed Martin
Published by Jenny Broom and Rachel Williams
Edited by Kate Davies
Production by Jenny Cundill and Kate O'Riordan

Manufactured in Guangdong, China CC1217

9 8 7 6 5 4 3 2 1